A&P
CREATIVE COOKING COLLECTION

Easy Meals for One & Two

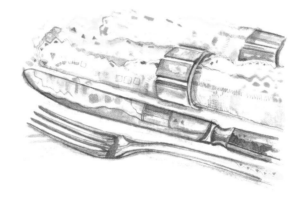

CREATIVE COOKING COLLECTION

Easy Meals for One & Two

Ann Page-Wood

CONTENTS

Published exclusively for Cupress (Canada) Limited,
10 Falconer Drive, Unit 8, Mississauga,
Ontario L5N 1B1, Canada
by Woodhead-Faulkner Ltd

First published 1987
© Woodhead-Faulkner (Publishers) Ltd 1987
ISBN 0-920691-14-5
Printed and bound in Singapore

INTRODUCTION

'It just doesn't seem worth all the bother' is the view expressed by so many people living alone to shopping and cooking for themselves. But, by planning ahead and shopping carefully, it is possible to produce an endless variety of dishes—making cooking a far more enjoyable task, and eating a pleasure. Whether cooking for one, two or a large family, it is equally important to aim for a diverse balanced menu.

With the growth of supermarkets and decline in the number of small grocery stores, etc. it became increasingly difficult to buy small quantities of ingredients. Recently, however, the food industry has recognized that bulk purchases are not suitable for every customer. More individual sized packs are now available, and supermarkets are introducing more self-service sections and delicatessen counters within their shops, so quantities can be selected to suit requirements.

The choice of equipment and dishes for small numbers is worth a mention. Small saucepans are obviously essential, but the divided saucepans which enable two or three items to be cooked separately and simultaneously on only one hotplate are well worth buying—for their fuel saving. Small flameproof dishes are also a worthwhile investment as they can be used under the broiler, in the oven or on the top of the range.

Cooking individual portions or meals for two can be rather expensive in a conventional oven, so it is worth considering purchasing a microwave oven or a dual purpose broiler/oven. Either can reduce fuel bills considerably.

The recipes in this book don't require specialized cooking or preparation techniques—the methods are simple and easy to follow—ideally suited to meals for one or two.

NOTES

Ingredients are given in both metric and imperial measures. Use either set of quantities but not a mixture of both in any one recipe.

All spoon measurements are level:
1 tablespoon = one 15 ml spoon
1 teaspoon = one 5 ml spoon.

Ovens should be preheated to the temperature specified.

Freshly ground black pepper is intended where pepper is listed.

Fresh herbs are used unless otherwise stated. If unobtainable dried herbs can be substituted in cooked dishes but halve the quantities.

Eggs are large size unless otherwise stated.

Freshly grated Parmesan cheese should be used where Parmesan cheese is specified.

ITALIAN PASTA

*50 g (2 oz) dried or 100 g
  (3½ oz) fresh pasta*
*8–12 basil leaves
  (depending on size)*
1 small clove garlic
1 tablespoon pine nuts
2 tablespoons olive oil
*2 tablespoons cottage
  cheese*

*25 g (1 oz) Parmesan
  cheese, grated*
*1 tomato, skinned and
  chopped*
*1 green onion, chopped
  finely*
2–3 black olives, quartered
salt and pepper to taste

Serves 1
Preparation time:
15 minutes
Cooking time:
15 minutes
Freezing:
Not recommended

1. Cook the pasta according to packet instructions; drain well and reserve 2 tablespoons of the cooking water.
2. Meanwhile, prepare the sauce. Finely chop the basil, garlic and pine nuts, then mix with the oil and cheeses. Stir in the reserved cooking liquid and heat gently.
3. Stir in the tomato, green onion, pasta, olives, and salt and pepper. Toss well and serve immediately.

SMOKED TROUT PÂTÉ

*175–200 g (6–7 oz)
  smoked trout*
1 lime, halved
*2 tablespoons natural
  yogurt*

*1 teaspoon horseradish
  sauce*
1 green onion, chopped
⅓ cup cottage cheese
pepper to taste

Serves 2
Preparation time:
10 minutes, plus
chilling
Freezing:
Not recommended

1. Remove the skin, head, tail and bones from the trout.
2. Cut a slice from one half of the lime and reserve for garnish. Squeeze the juice of the lime and place in a blender or food processor with the trout, yogurt, horseradish sauce, green onion and cottage cheese. Work until smooth. Season with a little pepper.
3. Transfer the pâté to 2 ramekins or a serving dish and chill for about 1 hour.
4. Garnish with the reserved lime and serve with warm crusty bread or toast triangles.

CRUNCHY CAMEMBERT SALAD

65 g (2½ oz) seedless
  grapes
2 celery sticks, sliced thinly
½ cup cashew nuts
125 g (4 oz) Camembert
  cheese
1 small radicchio

FOR THE DRESSING:
1 tablespoon wine vinegar
2 tablespoons olive oil
2 teaspoons snipped chives
pinch of mustard powder
salt and pepper to taste
TO GARNISH:
celery leaves

Serves 2
Preparation time:
15 minutes
Freezing:
Not recommended

1. Mix the grapes, celery and cashew nuts together in a bowl. Cut the Camembert into small pieces and add to the bowl.
2. Arrange a few radicchio leaves around the edge of 2 serving bowls. Cut the remaining radicchio into strips and add to the salad mixture.
3. Put the dressing ingredients in a jar and shake to blend. Pour over the salad and toss well.
4. Pile the salad into the serving bowls and garnish with celery leaves. Serve with crusty whole wheat bread.

CROUSTADES

These simple snack ideas can easily be made into more elaborate savouries to serve with drinks by piping the filling decoratively into the bread and garnishing with fresh herbs, gherkin fans, etc.

2 slices whole wheat bread,
  crusts removed
1 tablespoon butter, melted
⅓ cup cottage cheese
1 tablespoon natural
  yogurt

50 g (2 oz) cooked ham,
  chopped
2 pickled walnuts, chopped
1–2 teaspoons snipped
  chives
salt and pepper to taste

Serves 1
Preparation time:
5–10 minutes
Cooking time:
12–14 minutes
Freezing:
Not recommended

1. Flatten each slice of bread by rolling gently and evenly with a rolling pin. Brush one side with melted butter.
2. Press the bread, buttered side down, into 2 individual Yorkshire pudding tins. Brush with the remaining butter. Bake in a preheated oven, 200°C/400°F, for 12–14 minutes, until golden. Leave to cool while preparing the filling.
3. Cream the cottage cheese and yogurt together, then stir in the remaining ingredients.
4. Either spoon or pipe the mixture into the bread.

VARIATIONS

1. Mix 75 g (3 oz) fine liver pâté with 1 tablespoon finely chopped gherkins, 2 tablespoons natural yogurt, and salt and pepper to taste.

2. Mix 2 scrambled eggs with 2 teaspoons snipped chives and 25 g (1 oz) finely chopped cooked ham or smoked salmon. Spoon the mixture into the hot bread cases and sprinkle with paprika. Garnish with parsley.

PITTA PACKAGES

One pitta bread fully packed with a well-flavoured filling makes a very substantial snack, but if you are really hungry you can split the filling between two pittas.

125–150 g (4–5 oz)
  smoked mackerel fillets
  or peppered mackerel
  fillets
½ apple, cored and
  sliced
few lettuce or endive
  leaves, torn into pieces

1 or 2 pitta breads
FOR THE DRESSING:
1 tablespoon lemon juice
2 tablespoons natural
  yogurt
1 green onion, chopped
  finely
salt and pepper to taste

Serves 1
Preparation time:
10 minutes
Cooking time:
5 minutes
Freezing:
Not recommended

1. Cut the mackerel fillets into strips and place in a bowl. Add the apple and lettuce or endive leaves and mix gently.
2. Mix together the dressing ingredients; if using peppered mackerel don't include pepper. Toss the salad in the dressing.
3. Wrap the pitta bread in foil and reheat under a broiler for 3–5 minutes.
4. Pack the salad into the pitta bread to serve.

VARIATIONS

Try the following delicious variations or create your own fillings by experimenting with leftover ingredients.

SHRIMP AND AVOCADO
  FILLING
½ avocado, peeled and
  sliced
50 g (2 oz) peeled shrimp
few radicchio or lettuce
  leaves, torn into pieces
FOR THE DRESSING:
2 teaspoons lemon juice
1 tablespoon olive oil
1–2 teaspoons snipped
  chives
salt and pepper to taste

CHEESE AND DATE
  FILLING
1 small orange, sliced
few endive leaves, chopped
  roughly
2 dates, halved and stoned
1 tablespoon dry-roasted
  peanuts
1 green onion, chopped
25 g (1 oz) Cheddar or
  Double Gloucester
  cheese, diced

Mix the ingredients together for the chosen filling. For the shrimp and avocado variation, combine the dressing ingredients and toss the salad in the dressing. Continue as above.

EGG FLORENTINE

If you are unable to buy young spinach with very little stalk, increase the weight by about 125 g (4 oz) as the amount of waste on old leaves is considerable. Alternatively, use about 175 g (6 oz) frozen spinach.

250 g (8 oz) spinach	*1 tablespoon flour*
2 tablespoons cream	*175 ml (¾ cup) milk*
grated nutmeg, salt and	*3 tablespoons grated*
pepper to taste	*Parmesan cheese*
2 eggs	*TO GARNISH:*
FOR THE SAUCE:	*tomato slices*
1 tablespoon margarine	*parsley sprig*

Serves 1
Preparation time:
20 minutes
Cooking time:
3 minutes
Freezing:
Not recommended

1. Cook the spinach, with just the water remaining on the leaves after washing, for about 10 minutes, until just tender. Drain and chop roughly. Stir in the cream, and season well with nutmeg, salt and pepper. Keep warm.
2. Lightly poach the eggs until the whites are just set.
3. To make the sauce, melt the margarine in a pan, stir in the flour and cook for about 1 minute, stirring. Remove from the heat and gradually blend in the milk. Bring to the boil, stirring constantly, and boil for 1–2 minutes.
4. Stir in 2 tablespoons of the Parmesan cheese and season with salt and pepper.
5. Transfer the spinach to a lightly greased 600 ml (2½ cup) ovenproof dish. Make 2 hollows in it with the back of a spoon and place the eggs in the hollows. Pour over the hot sauce and sprinkle with the remaining cheese.
6. Cook under a broiler for about 3 minutes, until bubbling and beginning to brown. Garnish with tomato and parsley. Serve immediately.

RÖSTI

This traditional Swiss snack can be altered to use up any vegetables which you have available. For a more substantial meal, mix ¼ cup grated cheese into the potato mixture before frying.

200–250 g (7–8 oz)	*½ green pepper, chopped*
potatoes	*2 teaspoons sunflower*
4 teaspoons oil	*seeds (optional)*
3–4 green onions,	*salt and pepper to taste*
chopped finely	*coriander leaves to garnish*

1. Boil the potatoes for 10 minutes, until beginning to cook, but still firm. Drain and cool.

2. Meanwhile, heat half of the oil in a small non-stick frying pan. Add the green onion and green pepper and fry for 2–3 minutes.

3. Coarsely grate the potatoes into a bowl. Add the green onions, green pepper, sunflower seeds, if using, salt and pepper and mix well.

4. Heat the remaining oil in the frying pan, add the potato mixture and press down with the back of a spoon. Cook over a low heat for 15–17 minutes, until golden, turning once. Serve immediately, garnished with coriander.

Serves 1
Preparation time: 15 minutes
Cooking time: 15–17 minutes
Freezing: Not recommended

VARIATIONS

Cheese and Corn Rösti: Omit the green pepper and sunflower seeds and add ¼ cup grated old Cheddar cheese and 2–3 tablespoons cooked kernel corn to the potato and green onion mixture.

Bacon and Leek Rösti: Omit the onion, green pepper and sunflower seeds. Gently fry 2 slices chopped bacon and 1 small chopped leek before mixing into the grated potato.

MUFFIN PIZZAS

These little pizzas can be made with many different toppings. For a change, use crumpets (see below) instead of muffins as the pizza base.

2 teaspoons oil	*2 muffins, halved*
1 small onion, sliced	*8 tomato slices*
1 clove garlic, chopped finely	*125 g (4 oz) Mozzarella cheese, sliced thinly*
1 small green pepper, cored, seeded and chopped	*8 anchovy fillets, halved*
	4 black olives
1/4–1/2 teaspoon dried oregano	*salt and pepper to taste*

Serves 2
Preparation time:
15 minutes
Cooking time:
3 minutes
Freezing:
Not recommended

1. Heat the oil in a pan, add the onion, garlic and green pepper and fry for 4–5 minutes, until soft. Stir in the oregano and season with salt and pepper.
2. Toast one side of the muffins. Spread the untoasted sides with the onion mixture, top with 2 tomato slices, then a layer of cheese. Arrange the anchovy fillets in a lattice over the cheese and top with the olives.
3. Return to the broiler for 3 minutes or until the cheese is bubbling and beginning to brown. Serve immediately.

CRUMPET PIZZAS

2 teaspoons oil	*50 g (2 oz) cooked ham, cut into strips*
1 small onion, sliced	*75 g (3 oz) Cheddar cheese, grated*
1 clove garlic, chopped	
50 g (2 oz) button mushrooms, sliced	*salt and pepper to taste*
1/4 teaspoon dried oregano	*TO GARNISH:*
4 crumpets	*tomato strips*
2 teaspoons anchovy purée	*herb sprigs*

Serves 2
Preparation time:
15 minutes
Cooking time:
2–3 minutes
Freezing:
Not recommended

1. Heat the oil in a pan, add the onion and garlic and fry for 3–4 minutes. Add the mushrooms and cook for 2–3 minutes. Stir in the oregano, and salt and pepper.
2. Toast one side of the crumpets. Spread the untoasted sides with the anchovy purée, cover with the mushroom mixture, then top with the ham. Sprinkle with the cheese.
3. Return to the broiler for 2–3 minutes, until the cheese is bubbling and beginning to brown. Top each crumpet with tomato strips and herb sprigs. Serve immediately.

MUSHROOMS IN WATERCRESS SAUCE

A quickly made snack with a difference is always welcome.
This one has been enjoyed by several of my friends.

1 tablespoon butter
125 g (4 oz) button
  mushrooms, halved
FOR THE SAUCE:
65 g (2½ oz) watercress,
  chopped roughly
2 green onions, chopped
5 tablespoons boiling
  water

2 egg yolks
2 tablespoons milk
½–1 teaspoon lemon
  juice
grated nutmeg, salt and
  pepper to taste
TO GARNISH:
watercress sprigs

Serves 2
Preparation time:
15 minutes
Cooking time:
5 minutes
Freezing:
Not recommended

1. First, make the sauce. Place the watercress, green onions and boiling water in a small saucepan. Cover and simmer for 5–6 minutes. Leave to cool a little.
2. Beat the egg yolks and milk together.
3. Spoon the watercress mixture into a blender or food processor, add the beaten egg yolks and work until smooth.
4. Return the watercress sauce to a very low heat and stir constantly until it begins to thicken; do not allow it to boil or the sauce will curdle. Season well with nutmeg, salt and pepper, and lemon juice. Keep warm.
5. Melt the butter in a pan, add the mushrooms and fry gently for about 5 minutes.
6. Serve the mushrooms with the sauce poured over, either on toast, or with crusty whole wheat bread. Garnish with watercress sprigs.

HERRINGS IN OATMEAL

This is a variation of a traditional Scottish dish. The apple stuffing makes it a substantial supper dish.

1 herring, gutted
1 tablespoon milk
1–2 tablespoons Scotch
  oatmeal
1 tablespoon oil
FOR THE STUFFING:
2 teaspoons oil
1 shallot or small onion,
  chopped

1 small apple, peeled,
  cored and diced
1 teaspoon lemon juice
¼–½ teaspoon Dijon
  mustard
salt and pepper to taste
TO SERVE:
lemon wedges
herb sprigs

1. Cut the head and tail off the herring and slit from the head along the belly to the tail.

2. To make the stuffing, heat the oil in a small saucepan, add the shallot or onion and fry gently for 1–2 minutes. Stir in the apple, lemon juice and mustard, cover and cook gently for 5 minutes, or until reduced to a pulp.

3. Season the stuffing well, then spread it over one half of the inside of the herring. Fold the other side of the herring over and secure with cocktail sticks.

4. Dip the herring in the milk, then coat with the oatmeal.

5. Heat the oil in a large heavy-based frying pan, add the herring and fry for 10 minutes, turning once. Drain on kitchen paper. Remove the cocktail sticks.

6. Serve with lemon wedges and garnish with herb sprigs.

Serves 1
Preparation time:
15 minutes
Cooking time:
10 minutes
Freezing:
Not recommended

LENTIL SOUP

'Sweating' vegetables—cooking them in a covered pan over low heat—draws out their flavour without browning.

1 tablespoon butter
2 bacon slices, chopped
2 celery sticks, diced
1 carrot, diced
1 small potato, diced
1 onion, chopped
450 ml (1¾ cups) chicken stock

¼ cup split red lentils
4–6 tablespoons milk or cream
salt and pepper to taste
shredded celery leaves to garnish

Serves 2
Preparation time: 15 minutes
Cooking time: 25–30 minutes
Freezing: Recommended

1. Melt the butter in a saucepan, add the bacon and fry gently for 1–2 minutes. Stir in the celery, carrot, potato and onion and 'sweat' for about 5 minutes.
2. Stir in the stock and lentils, cover and boil for 10 minutes, then simmer for 15–20 minutes, until the lentils are cooked.
3. Transfer to a blender or food processor, add the milk or cream, and work until smooth. Season well with salt and pepper.
4. Reheat gently, then sprinkle with celery leaves. Serve with crusty bread.

LETTUCE SOUP

1 tablespoon butter
1 small onion, chopped
2 cups shredded lettuce
1 small potato, diced
300 ml (1¼ cups) chicken stock
5–6 tablespoons milk

squeeze of lemon juice
salt and pepper to taste
TO GARNISH:
2 tablespoons natural yogurt or cream
chopped mint
croûtons

Serves 2
Preparation time: 10 minutes
Cooking time: 25 minutes
Freezing: Recommended

1. Melt the butter in a saucepan, add the onion, lettuce and potato, cover and 'sweat' for 4–5 minutes (see above).
2. Stir in the stock, cover and simmer for 20 minutes.
3. Work in a blender or food processor until smooth.
4. Return to the heat, stir in the milk and reheat gently. Add the lemon juice, salt and pepper.
5. Pour the soup into warm bowls, stir a tablespoon of yogurt or cream into each and sprinkle with chopped mint. Pile a few croûtons on top and serve immediately.

SUNFLOWER SALAD

40–50 g (1½–2 oz) dried
  pasta shapes
105 g (3¾ oz) can
  salmon, drained and
  flaked
1 carrot, grated
½ small avocado, sliced
3 tablespoons kernel corn

few chicory leaves
FOR THE DRESSING:
2 teaspoons olive oil
2 teaspoons lemon juice
1 teaspoon each chopped
  fennel and parsley
salt and pepper to taste

Serves 1
Preparation time:
20 minutes
Freezing:
Not recommended

1. First, make the dressing: place all the ingredients in a small jar and shake well together.
2. Cook the pasta according to packet instructions; drain.
3. Gently toss together the salmon, pasta, carrot, avocado and corn. Pour over the dressing.
4. Arrange the chicory leaves around the edge of a serving plate to form the 'petals' of the sunflower. Pile the salad in the centre to serve.

PORK IN A CRUSTY COAT

1 egg yolk
1 teaspoon milk
2 tablespoons fresh
  breadcrumbs
2 teaspoons finely chopped
  mint

125–150 g (4–5 oz)
  boneless pork chop
1 tablespoon oil
1 small apple
salt and pepper to taste
mint sprig to garnish

Serves 1
Preparation time:
15 minutes
Cooking time:
10–15 minutes
Freezing:
Not recommended

1. Beat the egg yolk and milk together. Mix the breadcrumbs and mint together and spread on a plate.
2. Season the chop with salt and pepper, dip into the milk and egg yolk, then coat with the minted breadcrumbs.
3. Heat the oil in a frying pan, add the chop and fry for 10–15 minutes, turning once, until golden and tender. Transfer to a warmed serving plate and keep warm.
4. Meanwhile, core and slice the apple into rings. Quickly fry the apple slices until golden and tender. Drain on kitchen paper and arrange beside the chop. Garnish with mint and serve immediately, with seasonal vegetables or a mixed salad.

CURRIED LAMB

1 tablespoon oil
1 small clove garlic,
  crushed
5 mm (¹/₄ inch) slice fresh
  root ginger, chopped
¹/₂ teaspoon turmeric
¹/₂ teaspoon chilli powder
¹/₄ teaspoon ground
  coriander
¹/₄ teaspoon ground
  cumin
1 small onion, chopped

¹/₂ green pepper, cut into
  strips
150–175 g (5–6 oz) lamb
  neck fillet, cubed
2 teaspoons flour
150 ml (²/₃ cup) water or
  stock
2 tablespoons shredded
  coconut
salt to taste
coriander sprig to
  garnish

Serves 1
Preparation time:
10 minutes
Cooking time:
about 30 minutes
Freezing:
Recommended

1. Heat the oil in a saucepan, add the garlic, ginger, spices and onion and cook, stirring, for 2–3 minutes. Add the pepper and lamb and cook, stirring, for 4–5 minutes.
2. Sprinkle on the flour, then gradually stir in the water or stock. Cover and simmer for 15 minutes.
3. Add the coconut. Simmer, uncovered, for 8–10 minutes. Season with salt.
4. Garnish with coriander and serve with rice and a selection of side dishes.

STILTON-TOPPED STEAK

For a treat a Stilton-topped steak makes a superb meal. If time permits, marinate the steak for 2 hours, but this stage can be omitted if you need an instant meal.

150–175 g (5–6 oz) fillet
  steak
FOR THE MARINADE:
2 tablespoons red wine
1 tablespoon oil
¹/₂ teaspoon chopped
  oregano
1 clove garlic, sliced

FOR THE TOPPING:
40 g (1¹/₂ oz) blue Stilton
  cheese, crumbled
1 teaspoon horseradish
  sauce
1 teaspoon milk
salt and pepper to taste

1. First prepare the marinade, if using. Mix the ingredients together, pour over the steak in a bowl and leave in a cool place for 2 hours.
2. To prepare the topping, mash the Stilton cheese and horseradish sauce together. Moisten with the milk and season well with salt and pepper.

3. Drain the steak from the marinade, place under a broiler and cook for 5–6 minutes for a rare steak, 7 minutes for a medium steak, and 8–10 minutes for a well done steak, turning once.

4. Immediately spread the Stilton topping thickly and evenly over the steak.

5. Return to the broiler for 1 minute, until bubbling and beginning to brown.

6. Serve immediately, with a broiled tomato or mixed salad and crusty bread.

Serves 1
Preparation time: 10 minutes, plus marinating (optional)
Cooking time: 6–11 minutes
Freezing: Not recommended

DUCK WITH CRANBERRY SAUCE

1 tablespoon flour	1 tablespoon chopped
1 duck portion, weighing	green onion
about 350 g (12 oz)	75 g (3 oz) cranberries
1 tablespoon oil	5 tablespoons port
5 mm (1/4 inch) slice fresh	1–2 teaspoons sugar
root ginger, chopped	(optional)
finely	salt and pepper to taste

Serves 1
Preparation time:
10 minutes
Cooking time:
about 40 minutes
Freezing:
Recommended;
freeze the sauce
separately

1. Season the flour with salt and pepper and use to coat the duck.
2. Heat the oil in a saucepan, add the duck and fry for 10–12 minutes, turning once, until golden. Remove from the pan and drain off the oil and fat from the duck.
3. Mix the ginger, green onion, cranberries and port together in the pan. Add the duck, cover and simmer for about 30 minutes, until tender.
4. Transfer the duck to a warmed serving plate and keep warm. Transfer the sauce to a blender or food processor and work until smooth. Check the seasoning, adding sugar if you wish, and pour over the duck. Serve with a watercress or green salad.

TURKEY PIQUANT

125–140 g (4–4½ oz)	1 tablespoon redcurrant
turkey fillet	jelly
1½ tablespoons butter	2 tablespoons water
5 mm (1/4 inch) slice fresh	2 tablespoons chopped
root ginger, chopped	green onion
2 teaspoons corn starch	salt and pepper to taste
2 tablespoons frozen	shredded green onion
concentrated orange	(green part only) to
juice	garnish

Serves 1
Preparation time:
10 minutes
Cooking time:
8–10 minutes
Freezing:
Recommended

1. Cut the turkey fillet into strips approximately 1 cm (½ inch) wide.
2. Melt the butter in a small saucepan, add the ginger and fry gently for about 1 minute.
3. Season the corn starch with salt and pepper and use to coat the turkey. Add to the pan and fry for 1–2 minutes, stirring.
4. Stir in the remaining ingredients, bring to the boil, then cover and simmer for about 6 minutes until the turkey is cooked. Garnish with green onion to serve.

STUFFED HAM ROLL

2 teaspoons oil
1 shallot, chopped
25 g (1 oz) pre-soaked
   dried apricots, chopped
2 tablespoons whole
   wheat breadcrumbs
1/2 teaspoon chopped
   rosemary

1 orange
175–200 g (6–7 oz)
   unsmoked ham steak
pepper to taste
rosemary sprig to
   garnish

Serves 1
Preparation time:
20 minutes
Cooking time:
10 minutes
Freezing:
Recommended

1. Heat the oil in a pan, add the shallot and fry for about 4 minutes, until soft. Transfer to a bowl, add the apricots, breadcrumbs and rosemary and mix well.
2. Finely grate the rind of half the orange. Cut the orange in half, squeeze the juice from one half, reserve the other half. Mix 1 tablespoon of the orange juice and all the grated rind into the apricot mixture. Season with a little pepper.
3. Place the stuffing along the centre of the ham steak, roll the ham round the stuffing and secure with a cocktail stick or skewer.
4. Place in a flameproof dish and pour over the remaining orange juice. Cook under a broiler for about 10 minutes, turning occasionally.
5. Meanwhile, remove the peel and pith from the reserved orange half, then cut into slices.
6. Transfer the ham to a warmed serving plate, remove the cocktail stick and pour over any orange juice from the dish. Garnish with the orange slices and rosemary and serve with vegetables or salad.

KIDNEYS IN SHERRY SAUCE

1 1/2 tablespoons flour
2 or 3 lambs' kidneys,
   halved
1 tablespoon oil
1 bacon slice,
   chopped
2 tablespoons chopped
   green onion
1 small clove garlic,
   crushed
40 g (1 1/2 oz) mushrooms,
   sliced

2 tablespoons sherry
6 tablespoons chicken
   stock (approximately)
1/4 teaspoon chopped
   thyme
2 tablespoons frozen
   kernel corn
1 tablespoon cream
salt and pepper to taste
chopped parsley or thyme
   to garnish

1. Season the flour with salt and pepper and use to coat the kidneys. Reserve any remaining seasoned flour.
2. Heat 2 teaspoons of the oil in a frying pan, add the kidneys and fry until brown all over. Remove and set aside.
3. Add the remaining oil and the bacon to the pan, stir in the green onion, garlic and mushrooms and fry gently for 2–3 minutes. Stir in the remaining seasoned flour.
4. Pour the sherry into a measuring jug and make up to 125 ml (½ cup) with stock. Gradually add to the vegetables, then bring to the boil, stirring.
5. Lower the heat so the stock is just simmering. Return the kidneys to the pan with any juices which have run from them. Stir in the thyme and corn. Cover and simmer for 10–15 minutes, until the kidneys are cooked. Stir in the cream and check the seasoning.
6. Serve with noodles and garnish with parsley or thyme.

Serves 1
Preparation time:
20 minutes
Cooking time:
about 15 minutes
Freezing:
Recommended

BAKED TROUT

1 tablespoon butter	1/2 lemon, quartered
1 bacon slice, cut into	lengthways
strips	3 fennel sprigs
1 leek, sliced	3 tablespoons white wine
1 trout, cleaned	salt and pepper to taste

Serves 1
Preparation time:
20 minutes
Cooking time:
15 minutes
Freezing:
Not recommended

1. Melt the butter in a pan, add the bacon and fry for 1–2 minutes, until the fat begins to run. Add the leek and cook for 2–3 minutes. Set aside.
2. Make 3 slashes in each side of the trout and season well with salt and pepper.
3. Reserve one lemon wedge. Cut the peel and pith away from the rest and place in the cuts on one side of the trout with the fennel.
4. Place the leek and bacon on a large rectangle of foil, lay the trout on top and pour over the wine.
5. Fold the foil over to make a parcel and place on a baking sheet. Cook in a preheated oven, 180°C/350°F, for 15 minutes. A guide to determine whether the trout is cooked is the colour of the eyes: when they are white the trout will be cooked.
6. Transfer the trout and vegetables to a warmed serving plate. Serve with the reserved lemon wedge.

HALIBUT WITH VEGETABLES

Use cod or haddock instead of halibut if you prefer.

1 tablespoon butter	1 small zucchini, sliced
1 leek, sliced	175–200 g (6–7 oz)
2 carrots, sliced	halibut steak
3 tablespoons white wine	salt and pepper to taste
1/2–1 teaspoon chopped	1–2 fennel or dill sprigs to
fennel or dill	garnish

Serves 1
Preparation time:
5–10 minutes
Cooking time:
8 minutes
Freezing:
Not recommended

1. Melt the butter in a saucepan, add the leek and carrots and fry for 4 minutes.
2. Stir in the wine and fennel or dill. Cover with the zucchini and place the halibut on top. Season well with salt and pepper.
3. Cover and simmer for about 8 minutes, until the fish turns opaque; the cooking time will depend on the thickness of the steak, but do not overcook or the fish will spoil.
4. Garnish with fennel or dill and serve with potatoes.

AVOCADO SURPRISE

Most of us have eaten an avocado with shrimp as a starter. This recipe combines these two ingredients but serves them hot, topped with a cheese meringue, as a main course, although it could serve two as a starter.

1 small avocado
2 teaspoons lemon juice
75 g (3 oz) peeled shrimp
2 teaspoons chopped
  green onions
1 egg white

pinch of cream of tartar
25 g (1 oz) Parmesan
  cheese, grated
salt and pepper to taste
green onion to garnish

Serves 1
Preparation time:
10 minutes
Cooking time:
15–20 minutes
Freezing:
Not recommended

1. Cut the avocado in half lengthways and discard the stone. Using a teaspoon scoop out the flesh, keeping the skin intact. Dice the flesh.
2. Mix together the lemon juice, shrimp, green onions and diced avocado. Season well with salt and pepper.
3. Pile the avocado and shrimp mixture back into the avocado skins and place in an ovenproof dish.
4. Whisk the egg white and cream of tartar until soft peaks form, then gently fold in the Parmesan cheese.
5. Pile the meringue on top of the avocado and bake in a preheated oven, 180°C/350°F, for 15–20 minutes, until golden. Serve immediately, garnished with green onion.

LEEK AND CORN FRITTATA

A frittata needs cooking slowly over a very low heat so the eggs set gradually, unlike an omelette which is cooked very quickly over a high heat. The top of the frittata can either be cooked under a broiler or the whole frittata turned over and returned to the frying pan.

1 tablespoon butter
1 small leek, sliced
2 extra large eggs

2 tablespoons cooked
  kernel corn
2 teaspoons olive oil
salt and pepper to taste

1. Melt the butter in an 18 cm (7 inch) heavy-based omelette or frying-pan, add the leek and fry for about 5 minutes, until soft but not browned.
2. Beat the eggs lightly with a fork, add the leek and corn and season well with salt and pepper.

3. Heat the oil in the same pan, add the egg mixture and cook over a very low heat for about 12 minutes, until the frittata is set and the underside is golden brown.
4. Either slide the frittata onto a plate, cover with a second plate, turn over, slide the frittata back into the pan and cook for 4–5 minutes, or place the pan under a broiler for 2–3 minutes, to brown the top.
5. Serve with a crisp salad and whole wheat bread.

Serves 1
Preparation time:
10 minutes
Cooking time:
14–17 minutes
Freezing:
Not recommended

VARIATIONS
Replace the leek and corn with ½ red or green pepper, chopped, and ¼ cup grated old Cheddar or Gruyère cheese; or with 25–50 g (1–2 oz) chopped bacon, 1 small sliced zucchini and 1 tablespoon chopped green onion or chives. Proceed as above, pre-cooking the pepper, bacon and zucchini.

SPINACH AND AVOCADO SALAD

*200–250 g (7–8 oz)
   back bacon
175 g (6 oz) young
   spinach leaves
25 g (1 oz) pine nuts
1/2 avocado, sliced
50 g (2 oz) Danish blue
   cheese, crumbled*

*1 carrot, grated coarsely
FOR THE DRESSING:
juice of 1/2 lemon
3 tablespoons olive oil
good pinch of mustard
   powder
salt and pepper to taste*

Serves 2
Preparation time:
20 minutes
Freezing:
Not recommended

1. Cut the bacon into strips and fry in its own fat until crisp. Leave in the pan and set aside.
2. Tear the spinach leaves into small pieces and mix with the remaining salad ingredients in a serving bowl.
3. Shake all the dressing ingredients together in a screw-top jar. Pour into the pan with the bacon and heat gently.
4. Pour over the salad and toss well. Serve immediately, with plenty of warm crusty bread.

HAM WITH SPICY SAUCE

*2 tablespoons raisins
2 cloves
5 cm (2 inch) piece
   cinnamon stick
125 ml (1/2 cup) natural
   pineapple juice
1 tablespoon light brown
   soft sugar*

*1 teaspoon corn starch
1 tablespoon water
2 teaspoons lemon juice
2 ham steaks
salt and pepper to taste
orange slices to garnish*

Serves 2
Preparation time:
20 minutes
Cooking time:
6–7 minutes
Freezing:
Recommended for
the sauce only

1. Place the raisins, cloves, cinnamon stick and pine-apple juice in a small saucepan, cover and simmer for 10 minutes. Discard the cloves and cinnamon.
2. Blend the sugar and corn starch to a paste with the water, then gradually stir into the sauce and bring to the boil, stirring constantly. Stir in the lemon juice, and salt and pepper. Keep warm.
3. Cook the ham steaks under a broiler for 6–7 minutes, turning once. Garnish with orange slices and serve immediately, with the sauce.

CUMIN PORK

When fresh apricots are unavailable, substitute fresh chopped pineapple, peaches or nectarines. To skin the fruit, blanch in boiling water for 40 seconds.

1 tablespoon oil
1/2 teaspoon cumin seeds
200–250 g (7–8 oz) pork
    tenderloin, cut into
    1 cm (1/2 inch) slices
1/2 green pepper, cut into
    chunks
1 small onion, sliced
1/2 teaspoon ground
    cumin

5 mm (1/4 inch) piece fresh
    root ginger, chopped
    finely
1 teaspoon flour
150 ml (2/3 cup) pure
    apple juice
4 apricots, skinned, halved
    and stoned
salt and pepper to taste

Serves 2
Preparation time:
15 minutes
Cooking time:
15–20 minutes
Freezing:
Recommended

1. Heat the oil in a small saucepan, add the cumin seeds and fry until they start popping. Add the pork and cook, stirring, until it has lost its pink colour.
2. Stir in the green pepper, onion, ground cumin and ginger and fry for 2–3 minutes.
3. Stir in the flour, then gradually blend in the apple juice. Add the apricots, and salt and pepper.
4. Bring to the boil, then cover and simmer for 5 minutes. Remove the lid and simmer for a further 5 minutes. Serve immediately.

SWEET AND SOUR PORK

If you are in a hurry the marinating time can be reduced to 30 minutes, but the flavour will not be quite so good.

250 g (8 oz) pork
    tenderloin, cut into
    5 cm (2 inch) strips
75–125 g (3–4 oz) bean
    sprouts
FOR THE MARINADE:
1 tablespoon sherry
1 teaspoon soy sauce
FOR THE SAUCE:
2 teaspoons oil
4 green onions, cut into
    2.5 cm (1 inch) pieces

1/2 red pepper, cut into
    strips
2 teaspoons corn starch
125 ml (1/2 cup) water
2 teaspoons tomato paste
2 teaspoons light brown
    soft sugar
1 tablespoon wine vinegar
salt and pepper to taste
FOR THE BATTER:
1 medium egg white
1 1/2 tablespoons corn
    starch

1. Mix together the sherry and soy sauce for the marinade, pour over the pork in a bowl and leave to marinate for 1–2 hours.

2. To make the sauce, heat the oil in a pan, add the green onion and red pepper and fry for 3–4 minutes, until soft but not coloured.

3. Gradually blend the corn starch with the remaining sauce ingredients, stir into the pan and bring to the boil, stirring constantly. Remove from the heat.

4. To make the batter, mix the egg white and corn starch together.

5. Remove the pork from the marinade with a slotted spoon and set aside. Stir the marinade into the sauce.

6. Dip the pork into the batter and deep-fry in hot oil for about 3 minutes, until golden. Drain on kitchen paper.

7. Stir the pork and bean sprouts into the sauce and simmer for 2 minutes. Serve with buttered noodles or boiled rice.

Serves 2
Preparation time: 20 minutes, plus marinating
Cooking time: 10 minutes
Freezing: Recommended

LAMB CHOPS IN CIDER

This simple recipe combines the traditional favourites, lamb and mint. If you don't have anything else to cook in the oven at the same time, cook the chops in a covered pan on the lowest possible heat on the hob instead.

2 tablespoons flour
2 lamb chops, each
  weighing 175–200 g
  (6–7 oz)
1–2 tablespoons butter
1 onion, sliced
250 ml (1 cup) cider
175 g (6 oz) zucchini,
  sliced

1 small apple, peeled,
  quartered, cored and
  sliced
1 tablespoon raisins
2 teaspoons chopped mint
salt and pepper to taste
mint sprig to garnish

Serves 2
Preparation time:
20 minutes
Cooking time:
40–45 minutes
Freezing:
Recommended

1. Season the flour with salt and pepper and use to coat the chops. Melt the butter in a flameproof casserole, add the chops and fry until browned on both sides. Transfer to a plate.
2. Add the onion to the casserole and fry for 3–4 minutes. Sprinkle in any remaining flour and cook for 1 minute, stirring.
3. Gradually blend in the cider, then add the zucchini, apple, raisins, mint, and salt and pepper and stir well. Return the chops to the casserole with any meat juices, cover and cook in a preheated oven, 190°C/375°F, for 40–45 minutes, until tender.
4. Garnish with mint to serve.

MARSALA VEAL

2 veal escalopes, each
  weighing 100–125 g
  (3½–4 oz)
1 small onion, chopped
  finely
50 g (2 oz) button
  mushrooms, chopped
  finely
2 bacon slices, chopped
½ teaspoon finely chopped
  rosemary
6 juniper berries, crushed
1 teaspoon lemon juice

¼ cup fresh
  breadcrumbs
1–2 tablespoons milk
1 tablespoon butter
125 ml (½ cup) Marsala or
  sherry
3 tablespoons natural
  yogurt
salt and pepper to taste
2 teaspoons chopped
  parsley
rosemary sprig to garnish

1. Place the veal escalopes between 2 sheets of oiled waxed paper and, using a rolling pin, beat until they are very thin. Cut in half.

2. Mix together half of the onion, the mushrooms, bacon, rosemary, juniper berries, lemon juice and breadcrumbs. Season with salt and pepper and add sufficient milk to bind the mixture together.

3. Divide between the escalopes, roll up and tie securely with thin string or cotton.

4. Melt the butter in a small flameproof casserole, add the escalopes and fry for 3–4 minutes, until beginning to brown. Transfer to a plate. Add the remaining onion to the casserole and fry gently for 2–3 minutes, then stir in the Marsala or sherry.

5. Return the escalopes and any juices to the casserole, cover and cook in a preheated oven, 180°C/350°F, for about 1 hour, until tender.

6. Remove the escalopes from the casserole and discard the string or cotton. Arrange on a warmed serving plate.

7. Stir the yogurt into the sauce in the casserole and heat gently; do not boil. Pour over the escalopes and sprinkle with the parsley. Garnish with rosemary and serve with new potatoes, zucchini and carrots.

Serves 2
Preparation time:
30 minutes
Cooking time:
1 hour
Freezing:
Recommended at
end of stage 5

SPICED TURKEY PILAU

4 teaspoons oil
275–300 g (9–10 oz)
    turkey fillet, cubed
1 small onion, chopped
1 small red pepper, cored,
    seeded and sliced
1 small clove garlic,
    chopped finely
½ teaspoon cumin seeds
¼ teaspoon dried thyme

½ teaspoon turmeric
½ cup long-grain rice
2 tablespoons raisins
200 ml (1 cup) chicken
    stock
4 tablespoons natural
    yogurt
salt and pepper to taste
chopped parsley to garnish

Serves 2
Preparation time:
15 minutes
Cooking time:
15–20 minutes
Freezing:
Recommended

1. Heat 3 teaspoons of the oil in a pan, add the turkey and fry until it loses its pink colour. Remove from the pan.
2. Heat the remaining oil in the pan, add the onion, red pepper and garlic and fry gently for 3–4 minutes. Stir in the cumin, thyme and turmeric.
3. Return the turkey to the pan and stir in the rice, raisins and stock. Cover and simmer for 15–20 minutes, until the stock has been absorbed and the rice is cooked. Season with salt and pepper.
4. Stir in the yogurt and sprinkle with parsley to serve.

CANNELLONI IN STILTON SAUCE

175 g (6 oz) cooked
 chicken, diced
2 tablespoons chopped
 green onion
50 g (2 oz) mushrooms,
 chopped
1 tablespoon butter
1 tablespoon flour

175 ml (3/4 cup) milk
75 g (3 oz) blue Stilton
 cheese, crumbled
6 tubes dried cannelloni
2 tablespoons fresh
 breadcrumbs
salt and pepper to taste
parsley sprig to garnish

1. Combine the chicken, green onion and mushrooms.
2. Melt the butter in a small saucepan, add the flour and cook for 1–2 minutes, stirring constantly. Remove from the heat and gradually blend in the milk. Bring to the boil, stirring, then season well with salt and pepper.
3. Add 2–3 tablespoons of the sauce to the chicken mixture to moisten. Stir the cheese into the remaining sauce.
4. Stuff the cannelloni tubes with the chicken mixture and place in an ovenproof dish. Pour over the cheese sauce and sprinkle with the breadcrumbs.
5. Bake in a preheated oven, 190°C/375°F, for 25–30 minutes, until golden. Serve immediately, garnished with parsley.

Serves 2
Preparation time: 25 minutes
Cooking time: 25–30 minutes
Freezing: Recommended

SAVOURY CRUMBLE

2 teaspoons oil
1 clove garlic, crushed
1 onion, chopped
250 g (8 oz) ground beef
50 g (2 oz) mushrooms,
    sliced
213 ml (7½ oz) can
    tomatoes
½ teaspoon paprika

salt and pepper to taste
FOR THE TOPPING:
2 tablespoons butter or
    margarine
½ cup flour, sifted
¼ cup Cheddar
    cheese, grated
1 tablespoon sunflower
    seeds

Serves 2
Preparation time:
25 minutes
Cooking time:
20 minutes
Freezing:
Recommended

1. Heat the oil in a saucepan, add the garlic and onion and fry for 2–3 minutes. Stir in the beef and cook, stirring, until browned.
2. Add the mushrooms, tomatoes with their juice, paprika, and salt and pepper and stir well to break up the tomatoes. Cover and simmer for 5–6 minutes, then remove the lid and simmer for a further 5–6 minutes. Transfer to an ovenproof dish.
3. Meanwhile, prepare the topping. Rub the butter or margarine into the flour, then stir in the cheese and sunflower seeds. Sprinkle over the beef and cook in a preheated oven, 180°C/350°F, for 20 minutes. If necessary, place under a broiler to brown the topping. Serve immediately.

MOZZARELLA MEATBALLS

These meatballs should be cooked and served immediately, so that the Mozzarella cheese in the middle of each is just beginning to melt.

2 slices white bread,
    crusts removed
about 6 tablespoons milk
250 g (8 oz) ground beef
1½ teaspoons anchovy
    essence
½ teaspoon allspice
1 shallot, chopped finely
1 bacon slice, minced
25 g (1 oz) Mozzarella
    cheese, cut into 8
    cubes
1 tablespoon flour

2 tablespoons oil
salt and pepper to taste
FOR THE SAUCE:
½ cup tomato sauce
1 clove garlic
1 shallot, chopped finely
½ teaspoon chopped
    oregano
2 pinches chilli powder
TO GARNISH:
chopped oregano or
    parsley

1. Mix the bread with sufficient milk to make a paste. Stir in the beef, anchovy essence, allspice, shallot, bacon, and salt and pepper.

2. Divide the mixture into 8 pieces, roll each into a ball, press a cube of Mozzarella into each and roll again. Coat in the flour.

3. Place the sauce ingredients in a small saucepan, cover and simmer for about 15 minutes.

4. Meanwhile, heat the oil in a heavy-based or non-stick frying pan, add the meatballs and fry for 10–12 minutes, stirring constantly, until well browned on the outside but still slightly pink in the middle with the Mozzarella just beginning to melt. Drain on kitchen paper and arrange on a warmed serving dish.

5. Discard the garlic from the sauce. Pour the sauce over the meatballs, sprinkle with oregano or parsley and serve immediately.

Serves 2
Preparation time:
20 minutes
Cooking time:
15 minutes
Freezing:
Not recommended

SOLE WITH BANANA

The combination of fish and banana may seem rather strange, but they go together very well. I have used lime juice with the banana but if you prefer you could use lemon instead.

*2 tablespoons dried
   breadcrumbs
2 tablespoons grated
   Parmesan cheese
250 g (8 oz) sole fillets
1–2 tablespoons flour*

*1 egg, beaten
¼ cup butter
1 medium banana, sliced
   thickly
1 lime, halved lengthways
salt and pepper to taste
chopped parsley to garnish*

Serves 2
Preparation time:
15 minutes
Cooking time:
about 8 minutes
Freezing:
Not recommended

1. Mix the breadcrumbs and Parmesan cheese together, then season with salt and pepper.
2. Cut the sole into wide strips across the width of the fillet.
3. Coat with the flour, then the beaten egg, then the breadcrumbs and cheese. If necessary repeat the procedure to coat the fish completely.
4. Melt the butter in a frying pan, add the fish and fry for about 8 minutes, turning once, until golden. Transfer to a warmed serving plate and keep warm.
5. If necessary, add a little more butter to the pan, then fry the banana until golden.
6. Squeeze the juice from one lime half and stir into the pan. Pour over the fish.
7. Cut the other lime half into 2 wedges. Sprinkle the sole with chopped parsley and serve on warmed plates, with the lime wedges.

STUFFED MUSHROOMS

*175 g (6 oz) smoked
   haddock
bouquet garni of parsley
   and thyme sprigs and
   bay leaf
few peppercorns
4 large flat mushrooms,
   each about 8.5 cm
   (3½ inches)
   diameter
1 tablespoon butter*

*1 small onion, chopped
1 tablespoon chopped
   parsley
2 tablespoons whole
   wheat breadcrumbs
½ cup Cheddar
   cheese, grated
TO GARNISH:
lemon slices
parsley sprigs*

1. Place the smoked haddock in a pan, add the bouquet garni and peppercorns and cover with cold water. Bring to a gentle simmer and cook for 5 minutes. Remove from the heat and leave the fish in the pan to cool.

2. Meanwhile, remove any stalks from the mushrooms and chop them finely. Plunge the whole mushrooms into a pan of boiling water and boil for 3 minutes. Drain well on kitchen paper.

3. Melt the butter in a pan, add the onion and fry gently for 5 minutes, until soft. Add the chopped mushroom stalks and cook for 1 minute. Stir in the parsley, breadcrumbs and cheese.

4. Remove the smoked haddock from the pan with a slotted spoon and flake it into small pieces. Strain 1 tablespoon of the fish cooking liquid and add to the stuffing mixture with the flaked fish.

5. Divide the stuffing between the mushrooms, place in an ovenproof dish and bake in a preheated oven, 180°C/ 350°F, for 10–15 minutes, until crisp and golden on top.

6. Garnish with lemon and parsley to serve.

Serves 2
Preparation time:
20 minutes
Cooking time:
10–15 minutes
Freezing:
Not recommended

VEGETABLE TAGLIATELLE

125 g (4 oz) dried or 250 g
(8 oz) fresh tagliatelle
175 g (6 oz) broccoli
1 tablespoon butter
1 small onion, chopped

1 red pepper, cored, seeded
and cut into strips
2/3 cup cream
salt and pepper to taste

Serves 2
Preparation time:
20 minutes
Cooking time:
15–20 minutes
Freezing:
Not recommended

1. Cook the pasta according to packet instructions; drain and set aside.
2. Meanwhile, chop the stalk of the broccoli into small pieces; separate the florets. Set aside.
3. Melt the butter in a saucepan, add the onion and red pepper and fry gently for 3–4 minutes. Stir in the chopped broccoli stalk and cook for 1–2 minutes.
4. Add the broccoli florets, cover and cook gently for 10–15 minutes, until the vegetables are cooked but still crisp. Stir in the cream and salt and pepper. Stir in the tagliatelle and heat through. Serve with Parmesan cheese.

SPLIT PEA FRITTERS

50 g (2 oz) split peas,
soaked overnight
1 carrot, chopped
1 small onion, chopped
1 celery stick, chopped
1/4 teaspoon dried mixed
herbs

250 ml (1 cup) water
2 tablespoons flour
1 egg, beaten
salt and pepper to taste
TO GARNISH:
lemon slice
parsley sprigs

Serves 1
Preparation time:
10 minutes, plus
soaking and
cooking split peas
Cooking time:
5 minutes
Freezing:
Recommended

1. Drain the peas and place in a pan with the vegetables, herbs and water. Boil for 10 minutes, then cover and simmer for about 40 minutes, until the peas are tender.
2. Transfer to a blender or food processor, add the flour and work until smooth. If the purée isn't very thick, return to the saucepan and stir over a moderate heat for 1–2 minutes, then return to the blender.
3. Blend in the egg and season with salt and pepper.
4. Heat a little oil in a frying pan and fry heaped tablespoons of the mixture until golden brown on both sides. Garnish with lemon and parsley and serve immediately.

MIXED BEAN HOT POT

When boiling dried beans always add salt after boiling. If salt is added before cooking, the skin is toughened and boiling for hours will not soften them.

65 g (2½ oz) mixed beans
(e.g. red or white kidney
beans, black, pinto,
haricot), soaked
overnight
2 teaspoons oil
1 small onion, chopped
½ clove garlic, chopped
finely
50 g (2 oz) green beans,
sliced

50 g (2 oz) broad beans
150 ml (⅔ cup) tomato
sauce
4 tablespoons water
1 teaspoon chopped basil
15 g (½ oz) Cheddar
cheese, grated
salt and pepper to taste

Serves 1
Preparation time:
15 minutes, plus
soaking and
cooking beans
Cooking time:
20–25 minutes
Freezing:
Recommended

1. Drain the beans, cover with fresh cold water, bring to a rolling boil and boil hard for 10 minutes. Lower the heat, cover and cook for 40–50 minutes, until soft. Remove with a slotted spoon and set aside.
2. Heat the oil in a small saucepan, add the onion and garlic and fry gently for 4–5 minutes. Stir in the green and broad beans, tomato sauce, water, basil and cooked beans. Season well with salt and pepper, cover and simmer for 15–20 minutes.
3. Transfer to a warmed serving plate, sprinkle with the cheese and serve immediately.

EGG PLANT BAKE

Not all egg plants need to be 'degorged' but it is well worth salting them and leaving them to drain so bitter juices can run out before use. Do make sure you rinse them thoroughly before incorporating in any dish.

1 egg plant
2–3 tablespoons salt
1 tablespoon oil
1 small onion, chopped
½ green pepper, chopped
1 clove garlic, chopped
175 g (6 oz) tomatoes,
skinned and chopped
roughly

½ teaspoon chopped
marjoram
213 ml (7½ oz) can red
kidney beans, drained
2 tablespoons fresh
breadcrumbs
pepper to taste
marjoram sprig to garnish

1. Cut the egg plant in half lengthways and make 3 or 4 cuts along its length, not quite through to the skin. Rub the salt well into each incision. Leave the egg plant upside down to drain for about 30 minutes. Rinse thoroughly and squeeze gently.

2. Scoop out the flesh using a grapefruit knife and chop roughly. Set the shells aside.

3. Heat the oil in a saucepan, add the onion, green pepper and garlic and fry for 3 minutes. Stir in the chopped egg plant, tomatoes and marjoram, cover and cook gently for 5 minutes. Remove the lid and boil hard for about 2 minutes, to reduce the liquid.

4. Stir in the kidney beans and check the seasoning.

5. Divide the mixture between the egg plant shells, sprinkle with the breadcrumbs and place in a greased ovenproof dish. Bake in a preheated oven, 200°C/400°F, for 15–20 minutes, until the topping is crisp and golden. Garnish with marjoram to serve.

Serves 2
Preparation time:
25 minutes, plus standing time
Cooking time
15–20 minutes
Freezing:
Not recommended

STIR-FRIED VEGETABLES

1 tablespoon oil
10 blanched almonds
5 mm (1/4 inch) piece fresh
*   root ginger, chopped*
*   finely*
1 small clove garlic,
*   chopped finely*
1 small carrot, cut into
*   julienne strips*
1 small leek, sliced

1/2 red or yellow pepper,
*   sliced*
1 zucchini, sliced
75 g (3 oz) bean sprouts
1 teaspoon tomato paste
1 teaspoon soy sauce
1 tablespoon sweet sherry
2 tablespoons water
salt and pepper to taste

Serves 1
Preparation time:
15 minutes
Cooking time:
7 minutes
Freezing:
Not recommended

1. Heat the oil in a large pan, add the almonds and cook, stirring, until golden. Remove from the pan and set aside.
2. Add the ginger and garlic to the pan and fry for about 1 minute. Add the carrot, leek and red or yellow pepper and fry for 4 minutes, stirring constantly. Stir in the zucchini and bean sprouts.
3. Mix the tomato paste, soy sauce, sherry and water together, then pour onto the vegetables.
4. Increase the heat and boil hard for 2 minutes. Stir in the almonds, check the seasoning and serve immediately.

STUFFED ZUCCHINI

1 large zucchini, weighing
   200–250 g (7–8 oz)
1 tablespoon butter
2 tablespoons chopped
   green onion
4 tablespoons chopped red
   pepper
2 tablespoons almonds,
   chopped

½ teaspoon chopped
   marjoram
1 egg, beaten
¼ cup whole wheat
   breadcrumbs
40 g (1½ oz) Cheddar
   cheese, grated finely
salt and pepper to taste
marjoram sprig to garnish

1. Cut the zucchini in half lengthways. Scoop out most of the flesh, leaving a shell of about 5 mm (¼ inch). Chop the flesh.
2. Melt the butter in a pan, add the green onion and red pepper and fry for 4–5 minutes, until soft. Add the chopped zucchini and cook for 6–7 minutes, until soft. Stir in the almonds, marjoram, egg, breadcrumbs and half of the cheese. Season with salt and pepper.
3. Spoon the mixture into the zucchini shells and place in an ovenproof dish. Sprinkle with the remaining cheese and bake in a preheated oven, 190°C/375°F, for 20 minutes. Garnish with marjoram to serve.

Serves 1
Preparation time:
20 minutes
Cooking time:
20 minutes
Freezing:
Not recommended

SPINACH CROQUETTES

These croquettes are delicious served with the tomato sauce which accompanies Mozzarella Meatballs (page 40).

350 g (12 oz) young spinach leaves
1 tablespoon butter
3 green onions, chopped
¼ cup flour
125 ml (½ cup) milk
40 g (1½ oz) Cheddar cheese, grated

1 egg, beaten
20 g (¾ oz) pine nuts
½ cup whole wheat breadcrumbs
grated nutmeg, salt and pepper to taste
coriander leaves to garnish

Serves 2
Preparation time:
25–30 minutes
Cooking time:
6–8 minutes
Freezing:
Recommended

1. Cook the spinach, with just the water clinging to the leaves after washing, for about 5 minutes. Drain very well; press the spinach against the side of a colander, then squeeze it in your hands. Chop and set aside.
2. Melt the butter in a saucepan, add the onions and cook gently for 2 minutes. Stir in 2 tablespoons of the flour and cook over a low heat for 1–2 minutes. Gradually blend in the milk and bring to the boil, then simmer for 1–2 minutes, until the sauce is smooth but very thick. Add the cheese and remove from the heat. Season well with salt, pepper and nutmeg.
3. Stir in 1½ tablespoons of the beaten egg, the nuts, ¼ cup of the breadcrumbs and the spinach and mix well.
4. Divide the mixture into 6 pieces, shape into oblongs, then coat with the remaining flour, egg and breadcrumbs.
5. Fry the croquettes in a little oil for 6–8 minutes, until golden. Drain on kitchen paper and serve piping hot. Garnish with coriander and accompany with a salad and tomato sauce if you wish.

CARROT SOUFFLÉ

Serve this soufflé with a bowl of grated Parmesan or Gruyère cheese to sprinkle liberally over each portion.

175 g (6 oz) carrots, sliced or chopped
2 slices onion
1 tablespoon cream
1 tablespoon butter or margarine
2 teaspoons flour

6 tablespoons milk
1 teaspoon lemon juice
2 eggs, separated
grated nutmeg, salt and pepper to taste
grated Parmesan or Gruyère cheese to serve

1. Boil the carrots and onion in salted water to cover for about 15 minutes, until soft. Drain well and place in a blender or food processor. Add the cream and work until smooth. Set aside.

2. Melt the butter or margarine in a small saucepan, add the flour and cook, stirring, for 1 minute. Gradually blend in the milk, then bring to the boil, stirring.

3. Stir the carrot purée into the sauce with the lemon juice, nutmeg, and salt and pepper. Stir in the egg yolks.

4. Whisk the egg whites until soft peaks form, fold a little into the carrot sauce to lighten the mixture, then fold in the remainder.

5. Spoon the mixture into an oiled 900 ml (3⅔ cup) soufflé dish and bake in a preheated oven, 200°C/400°F, for about 25 minutes, until risen, set and golden brown.

6. Sprinkle a little grated cheese on the soufflé and serve immediately, with extra cheese and mixed salad.

Serves 2
Preparation time:
30 minutes
Cooking time:
25 minutes
Freezing:
Not recommended

STILTON SOUFFLÉ

1½ tablespoons butter or margarine	*2 teaspoons snipped chives*
2 teaspoons flour	*good pinch of mustard powder*
5 tablespoons milk	*1 egg yolk*
75 g (3 oz) blue Stilton cheese, grated	*2 egg whites*
	salt and pepper to taste

Serves 2
Preparation time:
15 minutes
Cooking time:
30–35 minutes
Freezing:
Not recommended

1. Melt the butter or margarine in a saucepan, stir in the flour and cook for 1 minute, stirring. Remove from the heat and gradually blend in the milk. Return to the heat and bring to the boil, stirring constantly.
2. Stir in the cheese, chives, mustard, and salt and pepper. Leave to cool a little, then stir in the egg yolk.
3. Whisk the egg whites until soft peaks form. Fold a little into the sauce to lighten the mixture, then gently fold in the remainder.
4. Spoon the mixture into an oiled 900 ml (3⅔ cup) soufflé dish and bake in a preheated oven, 190°C/375°F, for 30–35 minutes. Serve immediately.

OKRA CASSEROLE

Okra, or Ladies' Fingers as it is sometimes called, is a variety of green bean which has recently become popular in this country. If really young and tender, leave whole.

1 tablespoon oil	*350 g (12 oz) tomatoes, skinned and chopped*
1 clove garlic, crushed	
1 small onion, chopped	*½ teaspoon each paprika and chopped oregano*
½ green pepper, cut into strips	*4 tablespoons water*
175–250 g (6–8 oz) okra, cut into 2 cm (¾ inch) slices	*284 ml (10 oz) can lima beans, drained*
	salt and pepper to taste

Serves 2
Preparation time:
15 minutes
Cooking time:
25 minutes
Freezing:
Not recommended

1. Heat the oil in a saucepan, add the garlic, onion and green pepper and fry for about 3 minutes. Stir in the okra and cook, stirring, for 5 minutes.
2. Stir in the tomatoes, paprika, oregano, water, and salt and pepper, bring to the boil, then cover and simmer for 15 minutes.
3. Stir in the lima beans and simmer, uncovered, for about 3 minutes to heat through. Serve immediately.

STUFFED ARTICHOKES

Globe artichokes discolour very easily, so rub any cut leaves with lemon juice and avoid cooking them in aluminium or iron saucepans. When you have scraped out the choke, squeeze lemon juice into the centre to keep it looking fresh and white.

2 large globe artichokes
juice of ½ lemon
½ small apple, cored and
  diced
1 celery stick, chopped
213 ml (7½ oz) can red
  kidney beans, drained
1 tablespoon walnut
  pieces, chopped roughly

FOR THE DRESSING:
4 teaspoons olive oil
1 tablespoon wine vinegar
2–3 teaspoons snipped
  chives
salt and pepper to taste
TO GARNISH:
few chives

Serves 2
Preparation time:
20 minutes
Cooking time:
15–20 minutes
Freezing:
Not recommended

1. Cut the stalk off the artichokes and cut away the top third. Trim about 5 mm (¼ inch) off all the leaves and rub the cut surfaces with lemon juice to prevent browning.
2. Open the centre leaves and scrape out the choke, using a teaspoon.
3. Place the artichokes in a saucepan of boiling salted water, add any remaining lemon juice, and boil for 15–20 minutes, until tender. Drain upside down on kitchen paper and leave to cool.
4. Mix together the apple, celery, beans and walnuts.
5. Place the dressing ingredients in a screw-top jar and shake well to blend. Pour over the bean mixture and mix well, then pile into the artichokes. Garnish with chives and serve with warm crusty bread.

NUT CROQUETTES

1 tablespoon butter or
  margarine
1 tablespoon flour
4 tablespoons milk
1 teaspoon tomato paste
2 tablespoons shelled
  Brazil nuts, ground
2 tablespoons shelled
  hazelnuts, ground
2 tablespoons fresh
  breadcrumbs

15 g (½ oz) old
  Cheddar or Gruyère
  cheese, grated
salt and pepper to taste
FOR THE COATING:
1 teaspoon flour
1 tablespoon beaten egg
1–2 tablespoons dried
  breadcrumbs
TO GARNISH:
coriander leaves

1. Melt the butter or margarine in a small saucepan, add the flour and cook over a low heat, stirring. Gradually blend in the milk and tomato paste, then bring to the boil, stirring constantly.

2. Stir in the ground nuts, breadcrumbs and cheese, season with salt and pepper and leave to cool.

3. Divide the mixture in half and shape into rolls. Coat each croquette in the flour, then dip in the beaten egg and breadcrumbs.

4. Heat a little oil in a small frying pan and fry the croquettes for 2–3 minutes, until golden. Garnish with coriander to serve.

Serves 1
Preparation time: 20 minutes, plus cooling time
Cooking time: 2–3 minutes
Freezing: Recommended

SPICED PEAR

Cardamom is one of the oldest spices known to man. It was used by early Egyptians to keep their teeth white! Nowadays it is a major flavouring in curries and spiced cakes and pastries.

1 pear
juice of ½ lemon
seeds from 2 cardamom
  pods
6 tablespoons water

2 pieces preserved stem
  ginger, sliced thinly
4 tablespoons syrup (from
  the ginger)

Serves 1
Preparation time:
10 minutes
Cooking time:
10–15 minutes
Freezing:
Recommended

1. Peel and halve the pear; discard the core. Toss immediately in the lemon juice to prevent discolouration.
2. Place the pear and remaining ingredients in a small pan and poach gently for 10–15 minutes, until tender.
3. Transfer the pear to a serving dish, using a slotted spoon. Boil the syrup hard for 2 minutes, pour over the pear and leave to cool.
4. Serve with yogurt.

BANANAS IN ORANGE SAUCE

5 cm (2 inch) piece
  cinnamon stick
finely grated rind and
  juice of 1 orange
1 tablespoon light brown
  soft sugar

2 bananas
1 tablespoon Grand
  Marnier or Cointreau
  (optional)
2 tablespoons shredded
  coconut, toasted

Serves 2
Preparation time:
10 minutes
Cooking time:
4–5 minutes
Freezing:
Not recommended

1. Place the cinnamon stick, orange rind and juice, and sugar in a saucepan and heat gently, stirring occasionally, until the sugar has dissolved.
2. Cut the bananas in half lengthways, then in half widthways. Place in the orange sauce, cover and cook over a low heat for 4–5 minutes, until just tender.
3. Transfer the bananas to a serving dish. Remove the cinnamon stick and add the liqueur, if using, to the sauce. Pour over the bananas and sprinkle with the toasted coconut. Serve hot or chilled, on its own or with ice cream.

BLACKBERRY APPLE MERINGUE

Instead of the traditional meringue made with egg white and sugar, try folding in crushed ratafias—they impart a subtle almond flavour.

175 g (6 oz) apples
2 tablespoons water
1–2 tablespoons clear
* honey*

50 g (2 oz) blackberries
1 egg white
pinch of cream of tartar
25 g (1 oz) ratafias,
* crushed*

Serves 2
Preparation time:
15 minutes
Cooking time:
20 minutes
Freezing:
Not recommended

1. Peel, quarter, core and slice the apple and place in a small saucepan with the water and honey. Simmer gently for 3–4 minutes, until just beginning to soften.
2. Stir in the blackberries, then transfer to 2 ramekins.
3. Whisk the egg white with the cream of tartar until soft peaks form, then fold in the ratafias.
4. Pile the ratafia meringue on top of the fruit and bake in a preheated oven, 180°C/350°F, for 20 minutes, until golden brown. Serve warm or cold.

TROPICAL FRUIT SALAD

This fruit salad incorporates kiwi fruit, dates and kumquats. If you haven't eaten kumquats before they are well worth trying; eat the whole fruit, including peel and pips.

½ lemon
1 tablespoon sugar
2 tablespoons water
3 cloves
3–4 kumquats, halved
* lengthways*

1 kiwi fruit, peeled and
* sliced*
2–3 dates, halved and
* stoned*
1 teaspoon orange flower
* water*

Serves 1
Preparation time:
10 minutes, plus
cooling
Freezing:
Not recommended

1. Remove the rind from the lemon with a potato peeler; squeeze and reserve the juice. Place the lemon rind in a small saucepan with the sugar, water and cloves. Bring to the boil, stirring, until the sugar has dissolved. Remove from the heat and leave until completely cold.
2. Place the prepared fruits in a serving dish.
3. Strain the syrup into a jug, add the reserved lemon juice and the orange flower water, pour over the fruit and chill until required.
4. Serve with yogurt or cream.

RHUBARB FLUFF

If you prefer, gooseberries or apricots can alternatively be used for this dessert. It has a really special flavour.

175–200 g (6–7 oz) young rhubarb, cut into 2.5 cm (1 inch) lengths	*3 tablespoons sugar or to taste*
4 tablespoons freshly squeezed orange juice	*2 teaspoons gelatine 1 extra large egg white pinch of cream of tartar*

Serves 2
Preparation time:
15 minutes, plus
setting time
Cooking time:
4–5 minutes
Freezing:
Recommended

1. Place the rhubarb in a saucepan with 2 tablespoons of the orange juice. Cover and heat gently, allowing the juice to flow from the rhubarb, then simmer for 4–5 minutes, until soft.

2. Stir in the sugar until dissolved, remove from the heat and leave to cool.

3. Pour the remaining orange juice into a cup, sprinkle in the gelatine and stand the cup in a saucepan of simmering water until the gelatine has dissolved.

4. Purée the cooled rhubarb in a food processor or electric blender, or rub through a sieve into a bowl. Stir in the dissolved gelatine and chill until just beginning to set.

5. Whisk the egg white and cream of tartar until soft peaks form, then gently fold into the rhubarb purée. Spoon into a serving dish and chill until set.

6. Serve with crisp biscuits.

FRUIT BRÛLÉE

There are few desserts I enjoy more than fruit brûlée. It combines the fresh tang of fruit with the rich smoothness of an egg custard topped with caramel.

2 egg yolks	*few drops vanilla extract*
¼ cup sugar	*75–125 g (3–4 oz)*
125 ml (½ cup) whipping cream	*raspberries*

1. Whisk the egg yolks, 2 tablespoons of the sugar and 1 tablespoon of the cream well together.

2. Bring the remaining cream to the boil in a small saucepan. Leave to cool for 1–2 minutes, then whisk into the egg yolk mixture.

3. Strain the cream mixture back into a clean saucepan and stir with a wooden spoon over the lowest possible heat until the custard is thick enough to coat the back of the spoon. (Don't be tempted to hurry this procedure otherwise the custard will curdle.)

4. Leave the custard to cool for a few minutes, then stir in the vanilla extract.

5. Divide the raspberries between 2 ramekins, carefully pour over the custard and chill in the refrigerator for several hours.

6. Sprinkle the remaining sugar thickly over the fruit brûlées and place under a broiler for 1–2 minutes until the sugar has caramelized—take care not to let them burn.

7. Leave to cool, then chill before serving.

Serves 2
Preparation time: 15 minutes, plus chilling
Cooking time: 3–4 minutes
Freezing: Recommended at end of stage 4, if fresh fruit is used

VARIATIONS
Use other fresh fruit when in season, e.g. strawberries, blackberries, cherries, lychees. For a luxury version, add 1 teaspoon Grand Marnier or crème de cassis liqueur to the fruit in each ramekin.

WINTER FRUIT COMPOTE

The packets of dried mixed fruit now available are ideal for this dessert as they include apricots, prunes, peaches, apples and pears. If you wish, you could select two fruits and make a compote of your favourites.

75 g (3 oz) dried mixed fruit
5 cm (2 inch) piece cinnamon stick
finely grated rind and juice of ¹/₂ lemon

125 ml (¹/₂ cup) pure apple juice
¹/₂ teaspoon finely chopped fresh root ginger
1 tablespoon light brown soft sugar

Serves 1
Preparation time:
5 minutes, plus soaking time
Cooking time:
20–30 minutes
Freezing:
Recommended

1. Place the dried fruit, cinnamon, lemon rind and juice, and apple juice in a bowl and leave to soak overnight.
2. Add the ginger and sugar and transfer to a saucepan. Add sufficient water just to cover the fruit and simmer for 20–30 minutes, until tender.
3. Remove the cinnamon stick. Serve hot or cold with yogurt or cream.

RASPBERRY SOUFFLÉ OMELETTE

A soufflé omelette makes a filling dessert. This recipe uses raspberries, but most fruits could be used when in season, e.g. strawberries, peaches, apricots.

2 eggs, separated
2 tablespoons sugar
grated rind of ¹/₂ lemon

50 g (2 oz) raspberries
1 tablespoon butter
icing sugar, to finish

Serves 1
Preparation time:
10 minutes
Cooking time:
4–5 minutes
Freezing:
Not recommended

1. Whisk the egg yolks with all but 2 teaspoons of the caster sugar until light in colour. Whisk in the lemon rind.
2. Sprinkle the remaining sugar over the raspberries.
3. Whisk the egg whites until peaks form, then fold into the egg yolk mixture.
4. Melt the butter in an 18 cm (7 inch) frying pan, pour in the egg mixture and cook for 2–3 minutes, until the underside is golden brown. Place the pan under a broiler and cook for about 2 minutes, until the omelette is golden.
5. Arrange the raspberries along the centre of the omelette, fold the omelette over, and sprinkle with icing sugar. Serve immediately.

ENTERTAINING

These special occasion menus for two are ideal for intimate dinners.

MENU 1
Lettuce and Salmon Mousse
Lamb Noisettes Provençale
Minted Lemon Sorbet with Kiwi

MENU 2
Grapefruit Salad
Beef with Peppercorns
Simple Syllabub

MENU 3
Parma Pear Circles
Salmon with Asparagus Sauce
Mango Sorbet

MENU 4 (Vegetarian)
Tomato and Basil Ice
Vegetable Casserole
Chocolate Orange Mousse

MENU 5
Fried Camembert with Greengage Sauce
Poussins with Tarragon Sauce
Fruit Brûlée (page 60)

LETTUCE AND SALMON MOUSSE

*125 g (4 oz) coarse lettuce
leaves, chopped roughly
6 tablespoons white wine
1 1/2 teaspoons gelatine
1/2 × 105 g (3 3/4 oz) can
salmon, drained
50 g (2 oz) cream cheese*

*2 teaspoons lemon juice
1 tablespoon snipped
chives
salt and pepper to taste
lemon slices and chives to
garnish*

Serves 2
Preparation time:
20 minutes, plus
chilling
Cooking time:
5 minutes
Freezing:
Recommended

1. Place the lettuce and wine in a saucepan, bring to the boil, then simmer for 5 minutes. Leave to cool for a few minutes.
2. Strain 2 tablespoons wine from the lettuce and transfer to a cup or small basin. Sprinkle the gelatine into the warm wine and leave until dissolved.
3. Pour the remaining wine and lettuce into a blender or food processor, add the salmon and cream cheese and work until smooth.
4. Stir the dissolved gelatine into the salmon mixture, with the lemon juice, chives, and salt and pepper.
5. Transfer the mixture to 2 small jelly moulds or ramekins and chill until set.
6. To serve, dip the moulds quickly in hot water and unmould onto plates. Garnish with lemon and chives.

GRAPEFRUIT SALAD

If you use fresh broad beans for this recipe, 250 g (8 oz)
will yield about 65 g (2½ oz) shelled weight.

65 g (2½ oz) broad beans   *1 teaspoon snipped chives*
1 grapefruit   *1 tablespoon lemon juice*
75 g (3 oz) peeled shrimp   *salt and pepper to taste*
FOR THE DRESSING: *TO SERVE:*
2 tablespoons olive oil   *few lettuce, chicory or*
1 tablespoon clear honey   *endive leaves*

Serves 2
Preparation time:
20 minutes
Cooking time:
7 minutes
Freezing:
Not recommended

1. Boil the fresh or frozen broad beans in salted water to
cover for about 7 minutes, until their skins dimple. Drain
and slip each bean out of its waxy skin.
2. Peel the grapefruit, divide into segments and remove
the membranes, reserving any juices.
3. Mix the shrimp, beans and grapefruit together.
4. Place the dressing ingredients in a screw-top jar, with
any grapefruit juice, and shake well to blend. Pour over the
shrimp mixture and toss well.
5. Line 2 dishes with lettuce, chicory or endive leaves, and
divide the salad between them to serve.

PARMA PEAR CIRCLES

This recipe can be prepared several hours in advance,
then neatly sliced and arranged to serve.

1 large pear   *few lettuce or endive leaves*
1 teaspoon lemon juice   *FOR THE DRESSING:*
¼ cup cottage cheese   *2 tablespoons olive oil*
3 black olives, chopped   *1 tablespoon lemon juice*
2 teaspoons chopped   *¼–½ teaspoon Dijon*
*   walnuts*   *   mustard*
25 g (1 oz) Parma ham   *salt and pepper to taste*

Serves 2
Preparation time:
15 minutes, plus
chilling
Freezing:
Not recommended

1. Carefully remove the core from the pear, working from
the base. Sprinkle a little lemon juice in the cavity.
2. Mix the cheese, olives and walnuts together, spoon into
the cavity and chill for about 1 hour.
3. To make the dressing, place the ingredients in a small
screw-top jar and shake well.
4. Just before serving, slice the pear and cut the Parma
ham into neat pieces. Arrange alternately on a bed of
lettuce or endive. Pour over the dressing to serve.

FRIED CAMEMBERT WITH GREENGAGE SAUCE

This starter must be served as soon as the Camembert has been deep-fried. Don't try to keep the cheese warm or it will run out of its crisp coating.

125 g (4 oz) Camembert cheese
1 teaspoon flour
½ beaten egg
2 tablespoons dried breadcrumbs
mint sprigs to garnish

FOR THE SAUCE:
250 g (8 oz) greengage plums, halved and stoned
5 tablespoons water
1 tablespoon sugar
1 tablespoon wine vinegar
1 teaspoon chopped mint

Serves 2
Preparation time: 20 minutes
Cooking time: 45 seconds
Freezing: Recommended for the sauce only

1. Cut the Camembert into 4 portions and place in the freezer for 15 minutes.
2. Meanwhile, prepare the sauce. Place the greengages in a saucepan with the water and sugar. Bring to the boil, then simmer, uncovered, for about 10 minutes, until soft.
3. Purée in a blender or food processor. Stir in the vinegar and mint and keep warm.
4. Coat each Camembert portion with flour, then dip in the beaten egg and breadcrumbs. Dip once again in the egg and breadcrumbs to ensure the cheese is well covered.
5. Deep-fry the Camembert in hot oil for about 45 seconds, until golden. Drain on kitchen paper.
6. Garnish each portion with mint and serve immediately with the hot sauce.

TOMATO AND BASIL ICE

This is an unusual starter. It leaves a clean taste in the mouth and whets the appetite for the meal to come.

250 g (8 oz) tomatoes, chopped
1 celery stick, chopped
2 large basil sprigs
1 small onion, chopped
1 tablespoon sugar

1 tablespoon lemon juice
¼ teaspoon Tabasco (approximately)
1 egg white
pinch of salt
basil leaves to garnish

1. Place the tomatoes, celery, basil, onion, sugar and lemon juice in a small saucepan, cover and simmer for 15–20 minutes. Leave to cool.

2. Purée the mixture, including the basil sprigs, in a blender or food processor, then rub through a sieve.
3. Season the purée with the Tabasco; it should taste rather over-seasoned at this stage. Turn into a rigid freezerproof container, cover, seal and freeze for about 2 hours, until a 'slushy' consistency is obtained.
4. Whisk the egg white with a pinch of salt until soft peaks form. Fold a little into the half-frozen tomato purée to lighten the mixture, then gently fold in the rest. Cover, seal and freeze until firm.
5. Transfer to the refrigerator 30 minutes before serving to soften. Scoop onto chilled plates, garnish with basil and serve immediately.

Serves 2
Preparation time: 20 minutes, plus freezing
Cooking time: 15–20 minutes
Freezing time: 3 hours

LAMB NOISETTES PROVENÇALE

Serve with new potatoes cooked in their skins and French beans or zucchini.

1 tablespoon oil
4 lamb noisettes
1 clove garlic, chopped
  finely
1 onion, chopped finely
¹/₂ red pepper, chopped
  finely
300 g (10 oz) tomatoes,
  skinned and chopped

¹/₂ teaspoon chopped mint
¹/₂ teaspoon chopped basil
¹/₂ teaspoon sugar
salt and pepper to taste
mint or basil sprig to
  garnish

Serves 2
Preparation time:
15 minutes
Cooking time:
25 minutes
Freezing:
Recommended

1. Heat the oil in a saucepan, add the noisettes and fry for about 10 minutes, until golden. Transfer to a plate.
2. Add the garlic, onion and red pepper to the saucepan and fry for 3–4 minutes, then stir in the remaining ingredients.
3. Add the lamb and simmer, uncovered, for 10–12 minutes. Transfer the lamb to a warmed serving dish.
4. Boil the sauce rapidly for 1–2 minutes to reduce and thicken.
5. Spoon the sauce around the noisettes and garnish with mint or basil to serve.

VEGETABLE CASSEROLE

This casserole can be partially prepared in advance, then just brought to boiling point, topped with cheese and baked when required.

1 tablespoon olive oil
1 clove garlic, crushed
1 small onion, chopped
¹/₂ green pepper, cut into
  strips
175 g (6 oz) cauliflower
  florets
125 g (4 oz) zucchini,
  sliced
¹/₄ cup kernel corn
³/₄ cup tomato sauce
¹/₄ cup pearl barley

6 tablespoons water
1 teaspoon chopped basil
1 tablespoon chopped
  parsley
1 teaspoon paprika
213 ml (7¹/₂ oz) can red
  kidney beans, drained
125 g (4 oz) Mozzarella
  cheese, sliced
salt to taste
chopped parsley to garnish

1. Heat the oil in a flameproof casserole, add the garlic, onion and green pepper and fry for 3–4 minutes, until the onion is soft.

2. Add the cauliflower, zucchini, kernel corn, tomato sauce, pearl barley, water, herbs, paprika and salt. Bring to the boil and bubble for 1–2 minutes, then add the kidney beans.

3. Arrange the Mozzarella cheese over the top, cover and cook in a preheated oven, 190°C/375°F, for 35–40 minutes. Sprinkle with parsley and serve with baked potatoes topped with sour cream and chives.

Serves 2
Preparation time:
25 minutes
Cooking time:
35–40 minutes
Freezing:
Recommended

SALMON WITH ASPARAGUS SAUCE

Salmon always makes a delicious meal and serving it with an asparagus sauce makes it particularly suitable for a special occasion. Don't overcook the salmon or the texture will be spoilt. Frozen asparagus may be used for the sauce if the fresh vegetable is out of season.

2 salmon steaks, each weighing 150–175 g (5–6 oz)
125 ml (¹/₂ cup) white wine
bouquet garni of thyme and parsley sprig and bay leaf
few white peppercorns
1 slice lemon

FOR THE SAUCE:
125 g (4 oz) asparagus
2 tablespoons cream
squeeze of lemon juice
1 tablespoon butter
1 teaspoon flour
grated nutmeg, salt and pepper to taste
TO GARNISH:
lemon twists
parsley sprig

Serves 2
Preparation time:
20 minutes
Cooking time:
5–6 minutes, plus cooking asparagus
Freezing:
Not recommended

1. First, prepare the sauce. Cut any hard ends off the asparagus and gently scrape from the bud to the end of each stem. Tie the asparagus in a bundle and boil in unsalted water for 20–25 minutes, until tender; the buds should be above the water level and cook in the steam. If you don't have a saucepan large enough, halve the asparagus stems. Drain well.
2. Place the asparagus and cream in a blender or food processor and work until smooth. Add the lemon juice, and nutmeg, salt and pepper.
3. Melt the butter in a pan, stir in the flour and cook for 1 minute, stirring. Stir in the asparagus purée, then set aside.
4. Place the salmon in a saucepan with the wine, bouquet garni, peppercorns and lemon slice. Bring to a gentle simmer over a low heat and poach for 5–6 minutes, until tender. Transfer the salmon to warmed plates, using a fish slice, and keep warm. Strain the stock.
5. Reheat the asparagus sauce, thinning as necessary with the salmon stock. Pour a little sauce over each salmon steak.
6. Garnish with lemon twists and parsley. Serve with new potatoes and zucchini. Hand the remaining asparagus sauce separately.

BEEF WITH PEPPERCORNS

*250 g (8 oz) lean sirloin
    steak, cut into 2 cm
    (³/₄ inch) strips*
FOR THE MARINADE:
1 tablespoon oil
1 teaspoon chopped thyme
*1–1¹/₂ teaspoons green
    peppercorns*
125 ml (¹/₂ cup) red wine
1 clove garlic, sliced

FOR THE SAUCE:
175 g (6 oz) carrots
1 celery stick
1¹/₂ tablespoons butter
1 shallot, chopped
2 teaspoons flour
*2 tablespoons natural
    yogurt*
salt to taste
TO GARNISH:
thyme sprigs
celery leaves

Serves 2
Preparation time:
15 minutes, plus
marinating
Cooking time:
12–15 minutes
Freezing:
Recommended

1. Mix the marinade ingredients together, pour over the beef in a bowl and chill for about 2 hours.
2. Cut the carrot and celery into julienne strips.
3. Melt the butter in a saucepan, add the shallot and fry for 2–3 minutes. Stir in the carrot and celery, cover and cook for about 4 minutes.
4. Remove the beef from the marinade; discard the garlic slices but reserve the marinade.
5. Add the beef to the vegetables and cook, stirring, for 4–5 minutes, until the beef is well browned.
6. Sprinkle in the flour and mix well. Gradually stir in the reserved marinade, bring to the boil, then simmer for 2–3 minutes. Season with salt, then stir in the yogurt.
7. Garnish with thyme and celery leaves. Serve with brown rice and green beans.

POUSSINS WITH TARRAGON SAUCE

A poussin is a very young chicken, weighing about 350 g (12 oz). If you are short of time, broil—rather than bake—the poussins for 15–20 minutes, basting with the sauce.

2 poussins
*finely grated rind and
    juice of ¹/₂ lemon*
3 tablespoons olive oil
salt and pepper to taste
FOR THE SAUCE:
1 tablespoon butter
*1 tablespoon chopped
    green onion*

2 tablespoons flour
150 ml (²/₃ cup) milk
1 tablespoon lemon juice
*2 teaspoons chopped
    tarragon*
TO GARNISH:
tarragon sprig
lemon twists

1. Split the poussins by cutting them down through the breastbone. Open the birds out by bending back until the ribs crack, then cut in half.

2. Mix the lemon rind and juice, and oil together and season well with salt and pepper. Pour over the poussins in a dish and leave to marinate for at least 2 hours.

3. Transfer to a roasting tin and cook in a preheated oven, 180°–190°C/350°–375°F, for 30 minutes. Transfer to a warmed serving dish and keep warm.

4. Meanwhile, make the sauce. Melt the butter in a small saucepan, add the green onion and cook for 1–2 minutes. Stir in the flour and cook for 1 minute, stirring.

5. Gradually blend in the milk and lemon juice. Add the tarragon and bring to the boil, stirring constantly. Check the seasoning and pour over the poussins.

6. Garnish with tarragon and lemon twists. Serve with snow peas, baby carrots and baked potatoes.

Serves 2
Preparation time:
20 minutes, plus marinating
Cooking time:
30 minutes
Freezing:
Not recommended

SIMPLE SYLLABUB

Syllabubs date back to Tudor times when white wine or cider and fruit juice was sweetened, spiced with lemon or nutmeg, and milk added. This syllabub will separate after 4–5 hours, so don't make it too soon before serving.

1 lemon
2 tablespoons sweet sherry
1 tablespoon brandy
2 tablespoons sugar

grated nutmeg to taste
125 ml (¹/₂ cup) whipping
cream

Serves 2
Preparation time:
5 minutes
Freezing:
Not recommended

1. Pare about a quarter of the lemon rind with a potato peeler, then cut into thin strips. Reserve for decoration.
2. Finely grate the remaining rind and squeeze the juice from the lemon. Mix with the sherry, brandy and sugar, stirring until the sugar has dissolved. Add grated nutmeg.
3. Gradually whisk in the cream until the mixture is thick enough to hold its shape—do not over-whisk or the mixture will curdle.
4. Transfer to 2 serving glasses and decorate with a little grated nutmeg and the reserved lemon rind.

MINTED LEMON SORBET WITH KIWI

2 lemons
¹/₂ cup sugar
175 ml (³/₄ cup) water
2 large mint sprigs

1 egg white
pinch of cream of tartar
1 kiwi fruit, sliced, to
decorate

Serves 2
Preparation time:
25 minutes, plus
freezing
Freezing time:
3–4 hours

1. Pare the lemon rind with a potato peeler. Squeeze and reserve the juice.
2. Dissolve the sugar in the water over a low heat. Add the lemon rind and mint and boil gently for 10 minutes. Leave to cool.
3. Stir in the lemon juice, then strain into an ice cube tray or bowl. Cover, seal and freeze for 2–3 hours, until a 'slushy' consistency is reached.
4. Whisk the egg white with the cream of tartar until soft peaks form, then fold into the half-frozen syrup with a metal spoon. Cover, seal and freeze until firm.
5. Transfer to the refrigerator 10 minutes before serving to soften. Scoop or spoon into glasses and decorate with kiwi fruit.

MANGO SORBET

There is nothing quite like the taste of a mango and this sorbet is full of its flavour. Choose a really ripe mango which is turning golden yellow to make this recipe—for optimum flavour.

1 lemon
½ cup sugar
175 ml (¾ cup) water

1 very ripe mango
2 egg whites
pinch of cream of tartar

Serves 2
Preparation time:
25 minutes, plus cooling and freezing
Freezing time:
3–4 hours

1. Pare the lemon rind with a potato peeler. Squeeze and reserve the juice.
2. Place the sugar and water in a pan over a low heat and stir until dissolved. Add the lemon rind and boil gently for 10 minutes. Leave to cool.
3. Cut the mango either side of the stone and scoop out all the flesh into a blender. Add the lemon juice and work until smooth.
4. Discard the lemon rind from the syrup. Stir the mango purée into the syrup. Pour into a rigid shallow freezer-proof container, cover, seal and freeze for 2–3 hours, until-half frozen or 'slushy', stirring occasionally to break down the ice crystals.
5. Whisk the egg whites with the cream of tartar until soft peaks form. Gently fold into the half-frozen mango purée, cover, seal and freeze until firm.
6. Transfer to the refrigerator 10 minutes before serving to soften. Scoop into glass dishes to serve.

CHOCOLATE ORANGE MOUSSE

This simple mousse recipe is very adaptable. By replacing the orange rind, juice and liqueur with strong black coffee and Tia Maria, a delicious mocha mousse can be made. The recipe can even be halved quite easily for days when you feel like spoiling yourself!

75 g (3 oz) plain chocolate
finely grated rind of
*   1 orange*
2 tablespoons orange juice
2 eggs, separated
1 tablespoon Grand
*   Marnier or Cointreau*
*   (optional)*

pinch of cream of tartar
TO DECORATE:
chocolate curls (see
*   opposite) or toasted*
*   chopped hazelnuts*
2 tablespoons whipped
*   cream (optional)*

1. Break the chocolate into pieces and place in a bowl over a saucepan of simmering water until melted.
2. Stir in the orange rind and juice and egg yolks, mix well, then remove from the saucepan. Stir in the liqueur, if using.
3. Whisk the egg whites with the cream of tartar until soft peaks form. Fold a little into the chocolate to lighten the mixture, then gently fold in the rest. Spoon into 2 ramekins and chill until set.
4. Decorate the mousse with chocolate curls or chopped toasted hazelnuts and whipped cream, if you wish.

Serves 2
Preparation time: 20 minutes, plus chilling
Freezing: Recommended— open freeze, then seal in a freezer bag

TO MAKE CHOCOLATE CURLS
Using a potato peeler, shave thin layers from a block of chocolate at room temperature.

INDEX

Photography by: Clive Streeter
Designed by: Sue Storey
Home economists: Liz & Pete
Stylist: Gina Carminati
Illustration by: Linda Smith
Typeset by Rowland Phototypesetting Ltd